Table of Contents

My name is

Evan

My bird is the

American Crow It looks

like a flying butt it

Its color are black and

some selver It lives in

most of North Amerca

It eats fruitsand seeds.

fun fact birds are

like airplanes. Ther wings

act like airplane wings

and ther tales act like
prpelers.

American Robin has
brown legs. It
looks like a
baltimore reel.
It has an
orange belly,
yellow beak, and a
grey tail.

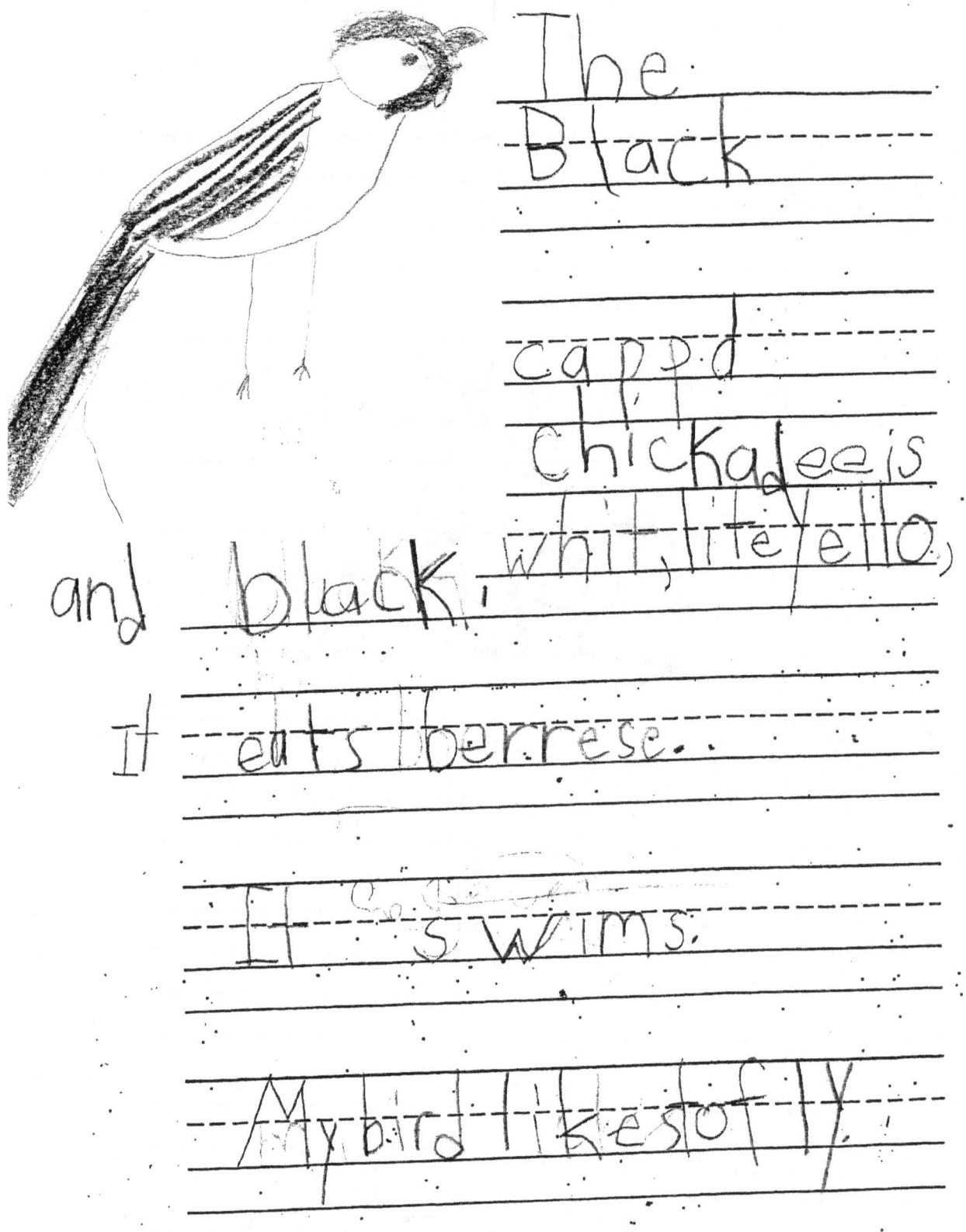

The
Black
cappd
Chickadee is
whit, life yello,
and black,
It eats berrese.
It swims
My bird likes to fly

It likes to eat.

It likes to billd a nest.

Its lase eggs.

It has good eay site.

feathers

beak

Cedar Waxwings
have light
yellow
bellyies and a grey
crest on thire head.
Cedar Waxwings got thire
name

from thire wing tips.

They look like they have

ben diped in red wax.

They are fonud in

New England. They eat

fruit and insects.

My bird
to ivs to fly
It eats ba-
ts, scwrlts, morning-
doves, mice, blue ja-
ys, robens, frog, chipmu-
nks and rabbits.

A Cooper's Hawks

colors are whit, gray,

black and oring. It lives in

the Forest, city, or in tow-

ns. The male is

smaller than the

female

My bird is a
Dark Eyed Junco.
It is metslle
black. It can fly. It has
a litol white on his
tall. It has a litel gray.

It can eat out of a brid
feeder. It has a wite
bele. It is wite, black and
gray. It has a black and
wite hed.

Downy

Woodpeckers

hav fiet and m

dark colors. They look

lik they hav a long

beak but they hav

a metiem beak. They
hav feathers on ther
beak. Males hav a pach of
red, females dont.

The House
Finch has
red on his
head. The nest
is made like a
cup. It eats

seeds and crumbs.

Dictated by Izadora to Miss Hunt

The House
Sparrow eats
worms and
bugs. It has
dark colors. They
are tiny. They

are brown on

top and a lot of

gray.

Dictated by Madison to Miss Hunt.

Mourning
Dove flys
rapidley and
is a member of the
pigeon family. It's
colors are red, white,

gray, black, tan and
brown. It has a small
head and a long tail
that comes to a
point. It lives in fields,
gardens or parks in a
in
tree or a shrub. It
eats almost all seeds.

My bird is a
Northern Cardinal.
Northern Cardinal's
are bright red.
Northern Cardinals make
ther nests very very high.

Northern Cardinals are
not scard of blue jas.

The PineGrosbeak
is
one of the
largist fichis.

The PineGrosbeak
lives in pair's.

It eats cranberry and
sunflower seeds.

The color is redish
and it is small.
It has a blak
curvd line behind its eye,
and it has a gray beak.

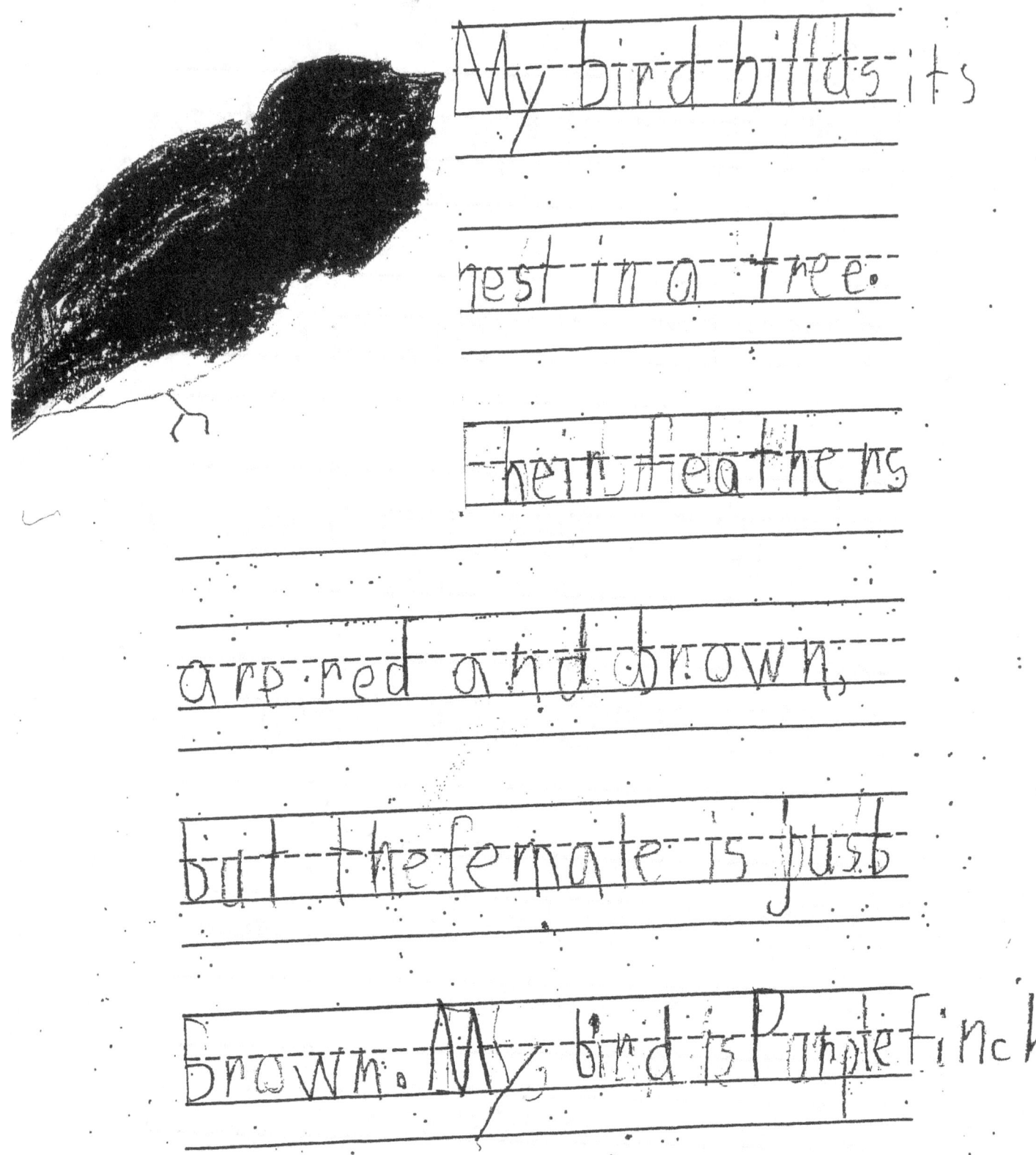

My bird bilds its

rest in a tree.

heir feathers

are red and brown,

but the female is just

brown. My bird is Purplefinch

It has a shanp beak.

It eats seeds. It's beak

piks up seeds. When the

chiks are old enuf

they can fly. It has

lats of colers.

Peck! Peck!

Peck! The

Red bellied

woodpecker hangs

on the tree and

pecks. It eats

bugs. It has

red low on its

belly. It has

long claws and

sharp nails. It

has a long beak.

Dictated by Eleanor to Miss Hunt.

My bird is
a Red-breasted
Nuthatch.

Their beely is
not anale red. It's
(actually,)
orinqe. It eats

insects *and* seeds. Their
nest
has *has*, fathers,
coft branches, and
sticky tree sap.
The
female weas a gray
The
cap. male weas a black
cap.

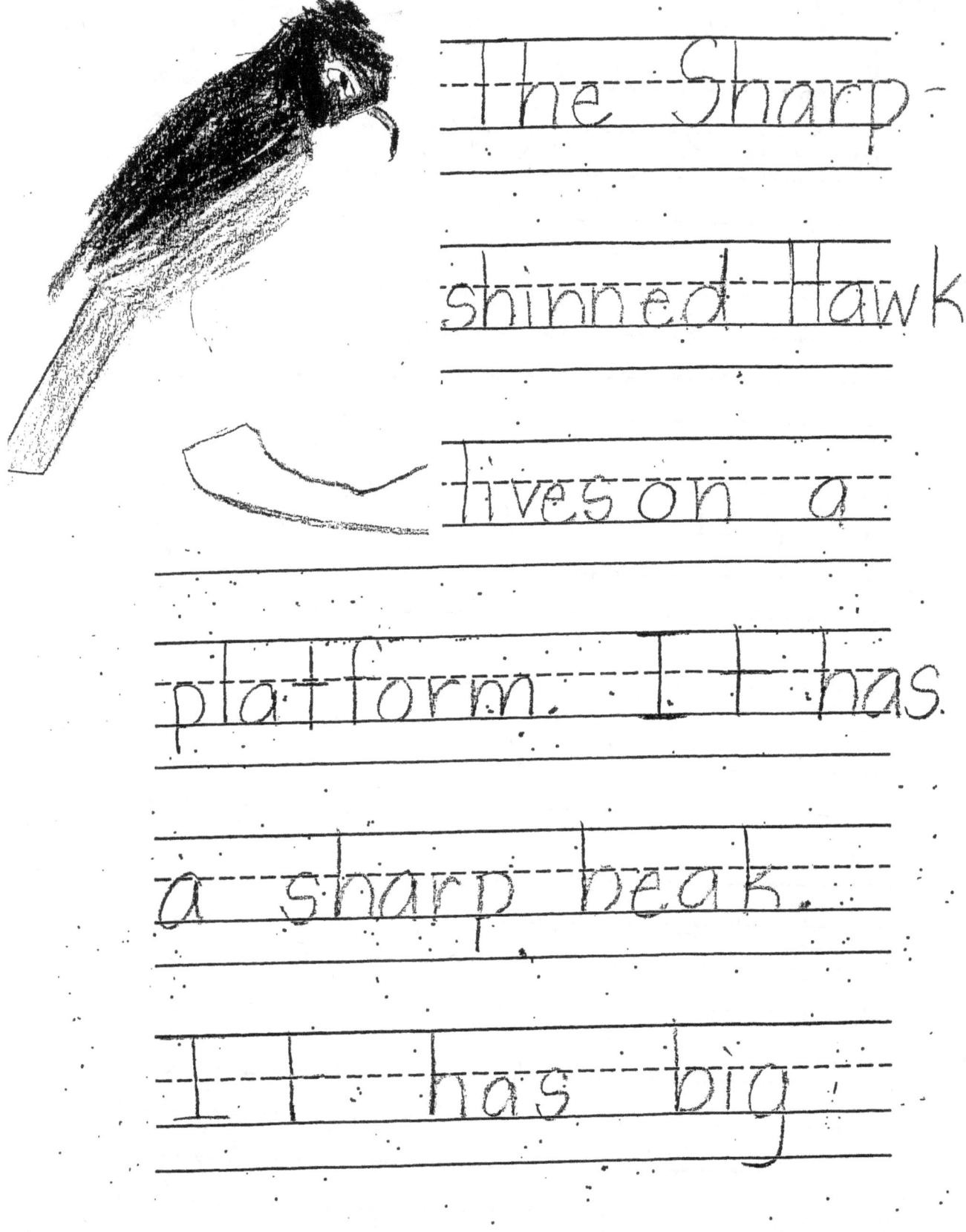

The Sharp-shinned Hawk lives on a platform. It has a sharp beak. It has big

claws. It is a
meat eater.

Dictated by Daniel to Miss Hunt.

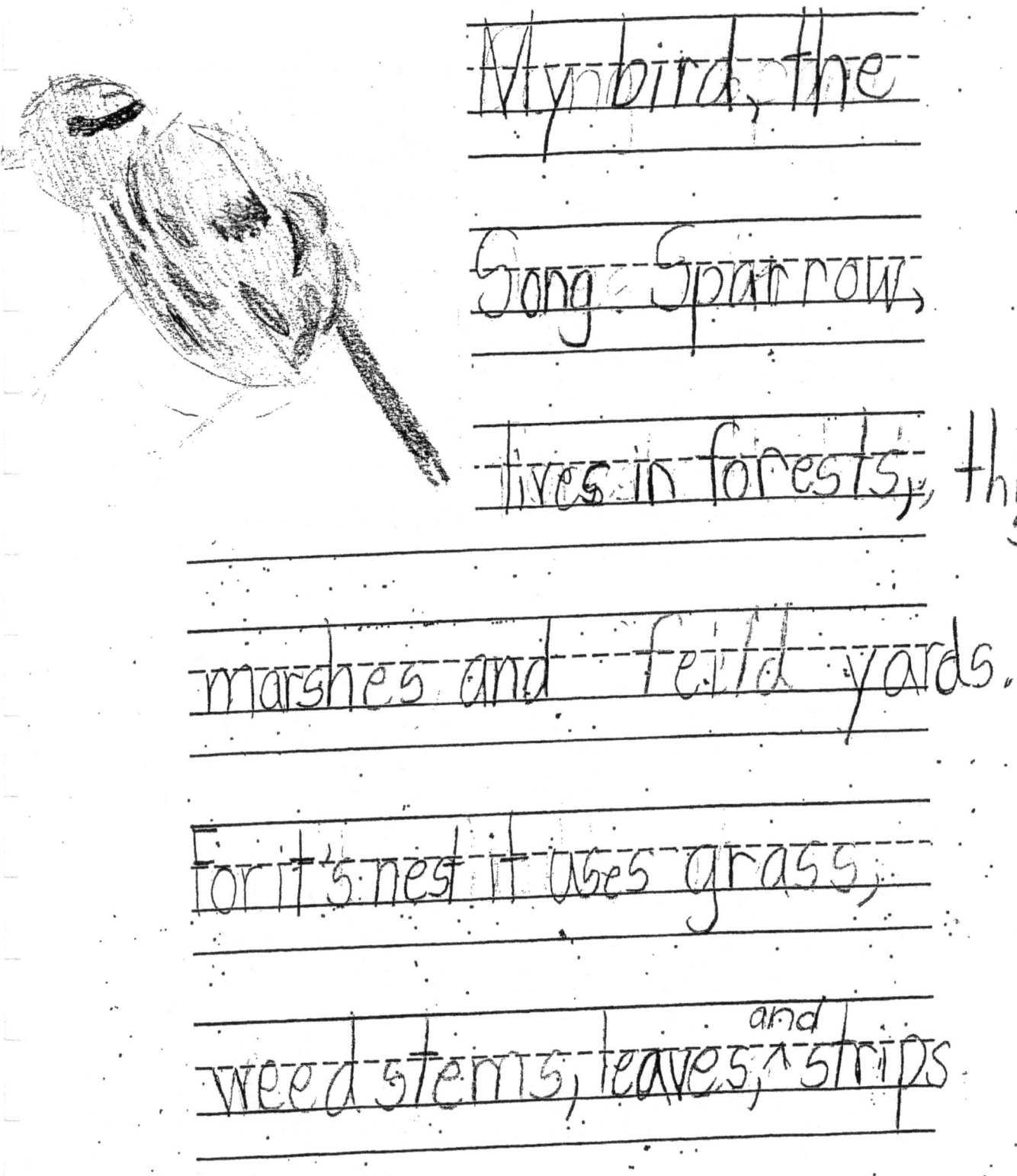

My bird, the

Song Sparrow,

lives in forests, thike
s

marshes and feild yards.

for it's nest it uses grass,

weed stems, leaves, and strips

of bark. It eats ins-
ects, seeds + fruit.

Also, the chicks have
a fast growth spurt
in there first week.

That's the Song Sparrow!

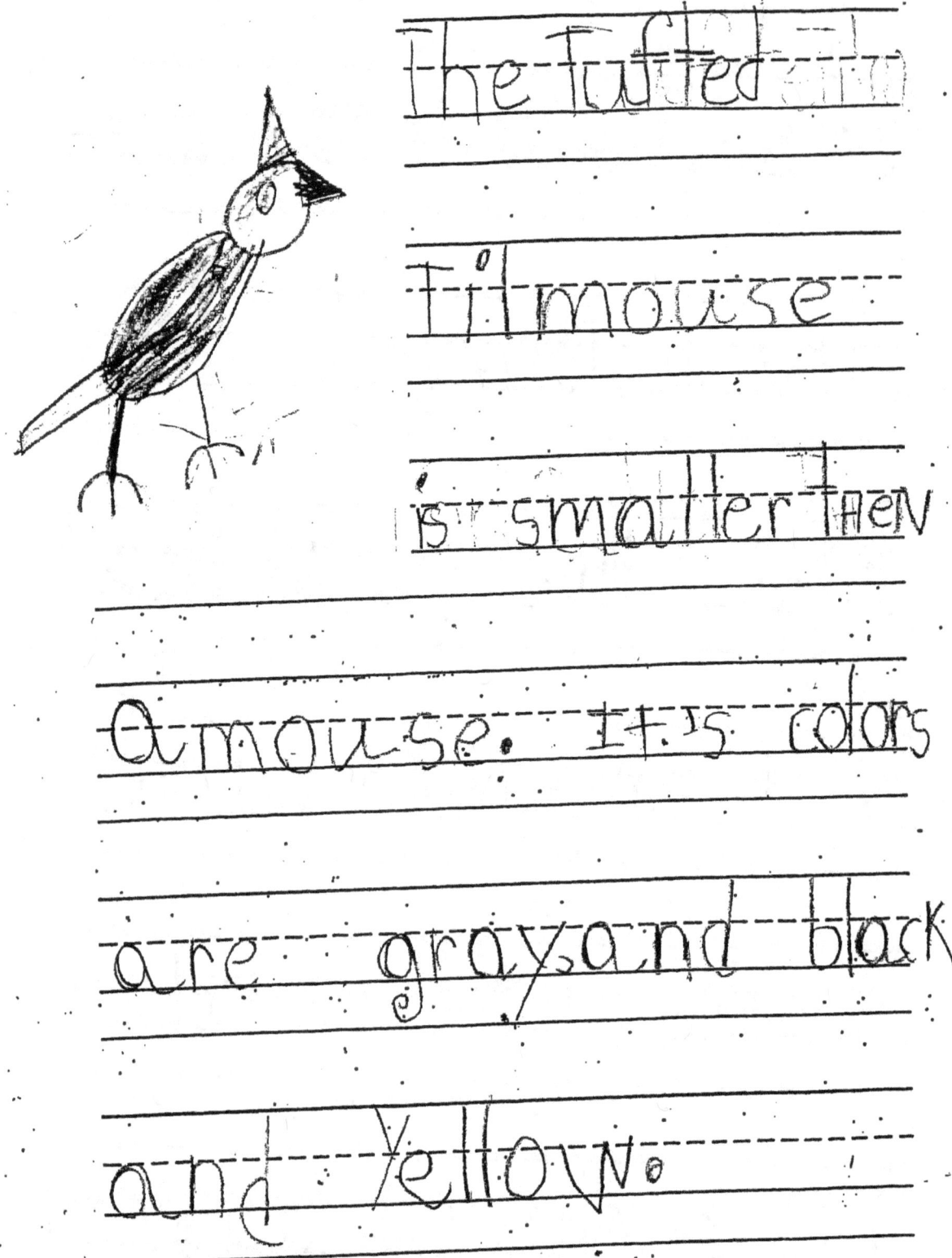

The tufted
titmouse
is smaller then
a mouse. It is colors
are gray and black
and yellow.

The Tufted Titmouse
Has a tufted crest
The Nest Is made
of meny
Materials.
It eats INsects
and berrIes.

It's big.

It's dagris. dangerous

And my bird is

the Wild Turkey has hen It

feathers. It eats corn.

It has spuclas.

It had black feathers.

It has black feathers.

It has big feathers.

It has a lite hed.

It has a bluw hed.

It has lite feet.

The white-
breasted
Nuthatch
has different
feathers going
different ways.

It is gray.

The beak is

kind of straight.

It eats seeds.

The face is

white.

Dictated by Jonathan to Miss Hunt.

the Yellow Rumped

Warbr looks

like a circt, utvat,

and a tine. The colors are

yellow, brown, and bla

ck. It livs hie plasys.

Aumost all warbrs' nests
are made with hay, but
some are made with stik
s. It can eat wroms, bugs
and seeds.